The Law Student's *Quick Guide* to Legal Citation

3d edition

D1490798

Steve Donweber

Boston University School of Law

Table of Contents

Introduction to Legal Citation

Legal citation is the method by which lawyers, law students, professors, and judges refer to the sources, whether primary or secondary,[1] that they rely upon when drafting court documents or legal memoranda, law school assignments, law review articles, and judicial opinions.

Citations are shorthand notations that permit the identification and location of a particular source. Elements of a citation generally include the identity of the source, where it can be found, the year it was created or went into effect, and for all primary sources and some secondary sources, the jurisdiction to which the source applies.

Because we rely on different sources for different reasons, legal citation also includes the use of **signals**, which introduce citations and explain to the reader the citation's purpose, and **explanatory parentheticals**, which follow the citation and provide further details on a source's relevance to the author's proposition.

Mastering legal citation takes practice, patience, and strict attention to detail. It means mastering the profession-wide standards for legal citation, which are set forth in *The Bluebook: A Uniform System of*

---

[1]   Primary sources include cases, statutes, and regulations. Secondary sources include hornbooks, monographs, legal encyclopedias, law review articles, and treatises.

Citation,[2] published by the Columbia, Harvard, and University of Pennsylvania Law Reviews, and the Yale Law Journal.

At its inception, *The Bluebook* was a modest undertaking designed only to "deal with the more common abbreviations and [citation] forms to which one has occasion to refer."[3] Needless to say, *The Bluebook* is modest no longer. It has grown from a 26-page pamphlet first published in 1926[4] to a 511-page behemoth when the latest edition (the 19th) came out in 2010.[5] This explosion in citation forms, rules, and complexity has made *The Bluebook* very difficult to use, particularly for new law students.

For that reason, I have put together *The Law Student's Quick Guide to Legal Citation*. Be forewarned; the *Quick Guide* is **not** comprehensive.[6] In terms of substance, it covers **only** (1) citing to cases, statutes, and secondary sources when found on Westlaw and LexisNexis, (2) the difference

---

[2]   This guide and its author are in no way affiliated with *The Bluebook* or any of the law reviews or journals that compile and edit it.

[3]   A UNIFORM SYSTEM OF CITATION 1 (Harvard Law Review ed., 1926).

[4]   *See id.*

[5]   *See* THE BLUEBOOK: A UNIFORM SYSTEM OF CITATION (Columbia Law Review Ass'n et al. eds., 19th ed. 2010) ("BLUEBOOK").

[6]   By design.

between citation forms in law review footnotes and those in legal memoranda and court documents, (3) abbreviations, (4) the use of signals and parentheticals, (5) basic citation forms for cases, statutes, and secondary sources, (6) citing to pocket parts and other supplements, and (7) short citation forms.[7]

I've limited the *Quick Guide*'s scope to avoid overwhelming the new student with a massive and confusing array of citation forms, abbreviations, and other rules that are seldom, if ever, used during the first year. Rather, I focus only on the areas (when it comes to legal citation) that I believe are most valuable to new law students.

Yes, *The Bluebook* is daunting, but it can be your friend if certain steps are followed and a certain proficiency is achieved.[8] I hope the *Quick Guide* helps. Good luck!

*   *   *

---

[7]   For everything else, you must, of course, consult *The Bluebook* itself.

[8]   This tidy bit of philosophy is based on something the Venerable Bede once said. Or, if not, really should have.

Using *The Bluebook*

It is important to understand *The Bluebook*'s purpose and its structure. Once you get those two things down, using *The Bluebook* becomes much easier.

As to *The Bluebook*'s purpose, or more generally, as to the purpose of uniform legal citation, it is twofold: (1) the identification of a source, and (2) where to find it. Judge Richard Posner, even though a harsh critic of *The Bluebook*, agrees:

> A system of citation forms has basically two functions: to provide enough information about a reference to give the reader a general idea of its significance and whether it's worth looking up, and to enable the reader to find the reference if he decides that he does want to look it up.[9]

This purpose is quite vital in both legal practice and scholarship.

How does knowledge of *The Bluebook*'s purpose help us use it? Well, if the purpose is to help us identify sources and then locate them, it's obvious that citation format, at least at its most basic level, must be standard and uniform. So, for example, every published United States case, whether state or federal, has the following format:

---

[9]   Richard A. Posner, *The* Bluebook *Blues*, 120 YALE L.J. 850, 852 (2011).

[case name], [volume number] [reporter in which case is published in print] [page number on which case begins] ([court that decided case][10] [year case was decided]).

Examples of case citations using this structure are below:[11]

```
    United States v. Pepperman,
    976 F.2d 123 (3d Cir. 1992).

 Costa v. Boston Red Sox, 809 N.E.2d
       1090 (Mass. App. Ct. 2004).

C.C.H. v. Philadelphia Phillies, 940
         A.2d 336 (Pa. 2008).
```

Due to uniform legal citation, we instantly recognize these examples as **cases** and we also immediately know, more specifically, where the case is published in print, the court that decided the case, and when the case was decided. This is very valuable information, and with uniformity, we get it at a glance.

The same principles apply to most other citation formats as well. The idea is that even if the specifics

---

[10]   For cases where the citation to the reporter clearly identifies the court (for example, Flood v. Kuhn, 407 U.S. 258 (1972)), there is no need to identify the deciding court in the parenthetical.

[11]   All citations in this *Quick Guide* are displayed using Courier font to show proper spacing.

of a citation are different, the uniformity in format permits easy recognition of the type of source, where to find it, and information about it.

As to *The Bluebook*'s structure, it pays to know where things are. *The Bluebook* is divided into four main parts. **First** are the so-called "blue pages," which provide typeface and citation format for court documents and legal memoranda (that is, for non-academic, non-law review related purposes). **Second** are the "white pages," which provide typeface and citation format for law review footnotes (that is, for academic purposes). Generally, the difference in citation format as between court documents and legal memoranda and law review footnotes (as shown in the "blue" and "white" pages, respectively) is typeface only. Citation structure as between the two is generally the same. The **third** part of *The Bluebook* is the domestic and foreign jurisdiction pages at Tables T1 and T2. These pages provide essential information as to citation preference and court and statutory abbreviations for specific jurisdictions. Finally, **fourth** are the general abbreviation pages, which begin at Table T6.[12]

The Bluebook also has an index, and a good one. Use it. For example, if you are wondering about the correct usage of the signal "see", just look up "see" in the index. Or, if you want to know how to (or even if you should) cite to a case's subsequent history, again just look up "subsequent history." You'll be quickly directed to the right place.

---

[12]   For more on abbreviations, see page 16.

Finally, much tedium can be avoided by simply looking at the inside front or back covers of *The Bluebook*, which contain quick reference guides for most common citation forms and can provide answers to many basic citation questions without very much effort at all.

*   *   *

Essential Bluebooking Tips

Everyone using *The Bluebook* should be aware of the following:

1.   **Print v. Online.** If the source you are citing to is available in print, you must cite to the source as if you found it in print (with some exceptions), *even if you found the source online*. With the exception of citation to cases, this requires checking the actual print volume for, among other things, the year of publication of the print source.

2.   **Year of the Code for Statutes.** Proper citation requires that all cites to a statutory code section contain the year of publication of the code. This means the year of the code as published *in print*. You must always provide the year of the code as published in print even if you found your particular code section online. This means that you always have to check the appropriate print volume of the code to find the correct year. For more information on finding the year of the code, see pages 41-46.

3.   **Year of Publication for Non-Periodical Secondary Sources.** Non-periodical secondary sources include treatises, practice guides, hornbooks, legal encyclopedias, and dictionaries. As with statutory codes, even if you find a particular non-periodical secondary source online, you must find the appropriate print volume to determine the correct year of publication. Generally, you will find

the year of publication on the book's copyright page. For more on this, see page 50.

4. **Citing to Supplements and Pocket Parts.** As noted above, if the cited source is found in print, you must cite to the print version. If relevant material in the print source is found in a pocket part or supplement, you must cite to the pocket part or supplement in addition to the main volume. For more on this, see pages 60-63.

5. **Abbreviations.** You must abbreviate words in your citations the way *The Bluebook* tells you. This means using the tables that form the latter half of *The Bluebook*. For more on abbreviations, see page 16.

6. **Parallel Citations**. Unless you are told otherwise by your instructor, do *not* use parallel citations when citing to the decisions of state courts. Use of the regional reporter only is preferred. For more on this, see page 32.

7. **Preferred Source.** Not only does Table T1 of the Bluebook contain abbreviations for courts and reporters, it also contains the preferred source to use when citing to cases, statutes, or regulations. For example, even though state court cases are found in several different reporters, *The Bluebook* prefers that you cite to the print regional reporter only if the case is found therein. The same type of thing goes for statutes and regulations, which have their own preferred sources, so always check Table T1 to determine the preferred source for citation.

Citing to Cases, Statutes, and Secondary Sources that You Find on Westlaw and LexisNexis

The general rule when citing to materials that you find on Westlaw or LexisNexis is this: if the resource is published in print, *always* cite to it *as if you found it in print*. This does not present a problem for cases, because the authoritative citation to the print version of a case is nearly always supplied when you view the case online.

Not so, unfortunately, with statutes and non-periodical secondary sources.[13] With statutes and non-periodical secondary sources, the online databases do not supply the authoritative **year of the code** for statutes or the authoritative **year of publication** for non-periodical secondary sources, both of which are required for proper citation.

The solution? Even if you have used the online version of a statute or non-periodical secondary source, to cite it properly, you *must* go to the print version and find the proper year of the code or year of publication.[14]

---

[13]   Non-periodical secondary sources include treatises, practice guides, hornbooks, legal encyclopedias, and dictionaries. As for periodicals like journals, magazines, and newspapers, you should be able to find the proper year of publication online.

[14]   **Note:** For non-periodical secondary sources, the year of publication is generally on the copyright page. For a

Law Review Footnotes v. Court Documents and Legal Memoranda

As mentioned above, there are differences in typeface conventions for citations in court documents and legal memoranda (non-academic citation) *and* for those in law review footnotes (academic citation). These differences can generally be described as Blue Pages v. White Pages because it's the Blue Pages at the beginning of *The Bluebook* that contain the formats for citations used in court documents and legal memoranda, and it's the White Pages that come next that contain the formats for citations appearing in law review footnotes.

The key distinction between citing according to the Blue Pages and the White Pages is TYPEFACE. By that I mean usage of *italics*, <u>underlining</u>, LARGE AND SMALL CAPITALS, and regular roman type. The typeface distinction is generally the only difference between the two formats. So, you can use the White Pages to guide you when citing in court documents and legal memoranda so long as you use the correct typeface.

Here are three examples, showing the forms for both academic and non-academic citation.[15]

---

discussion on finding the proper year of the code, see pages 41-46.

[15] Please note: Even though *The Bluebook* permits the use of italics **instead of** underlining in court documents and legal memoranda where appropriate (*see* Rule B1, at 3), I don't recommend italicization in non-academic citation for three

Case Names. In law review footnotes, case names are in regular roman type when used in a citation and *italicized* when the case name is an actual grammatical part of a sentence.[16]

Here's what we mean by using a case name in a citation (in this case, in a footnote).

> The Supreme Court has often discussed the territorial limits placed on a court's jurisdiction. *See, e.g.*, Pennoyer v. Neff, 95 U.S. 714 (1878).

Here's what we mean by using a case name as a grammatical part of a sentence.

> In *Pennoyer v. Neff*, the Supreme Court outlined a power theory of personal jurisdiction.

By contrast, in the actual text of the law review article (that is, not in a footnote) the case name is always *italicized*.[17]

---

reasons: (1) judges are likely accustomed to seeing underlining in court documents as that has been the long-time standard (the choice of italics is new); (2) it is my belief that students would find a failure to distinguish between the two formats confusing in the learning process; and perhaps most importantly, (3) every relevant example given in the Blue Pages for non-academic citation is underlined; none are italicized. And, as I consider examples to be a vital part of using *The Bluebook*, I'll use underlining for my Blue Pages, non-academic examples as well.

[16]   *See* BLUEBOOK, *supra* note 5, at 63-4.

[17]   *See id.* at 64.

In court documents and legal memoranda, case names are <u>underlined</u>,[18] whether in the text or in a footnote.[19]

Below are examples of the application of these rules.

In text of law review article or as grammatical part of sentence in law review footnote.

Pennoyer v. Neff

In law review footnote as citation.

Pennoyer v. Neff, 95 U.S. 714 (1878).

In a court document or legal memorandum.

<u>Pennoyer v. Neff</u>, 95 U.S. 714 (1878).

---

[18]   Although italicization is permitted, I don't recommend it. *See supra* note 15.

[19]   *See* BLUEBOOK, *supra* note 5, at 4.

Books. In law review footnotes, books are placed in large and small capital letters.[20] In court documents and legal memoranda, the title of the book is underlined and other aspects of the citation are in regular roman type.[21] Below are examples.

In law review footnote.

JONATHAN STROUD, THE AMULET OF SAMARKAND (2003).

In court document or legal memorandum.

Jonathan Stroud, <u>The Amulet of Samarkand</u> (2003).

Court Rules. Court rules are cited using large and small caps in law review footnotes and regular roman type in court documents and legal memoranda.[22] Below are examples.

In law review footnote.

FED. R. CIV. P. 12(b)(6).

In court document or legal memorandum.

Fed. R. Civ. P. 12(b)(6).

---

[20]   *Id.* at 63.

[21]   *Id.* at 23.

[22]   *Id.* at 17, 121.

In all three examples, please notice that the structure of the citation (elements of the citation, abbreviations, spacing, etc.) remains the same whether in a law review footnote or court document and legal memorandum. The only difference is the typeface.

*   *   *

Abbreviations

The Bluebook is huge into **abbreviations**. Every court has an abbreviation, every reporter has an abbreviation, every law review has an abbreviation, and many ordinary words are also abbreviated in case names and the like pursuant to *The Bluebook*'s voluminous abbreviation tables (the abbreviation tables are the blue edged pages that essentially compose the second half of *The Bluebook*).

Here's how the abbreviation rules and tables are structured.

The general rules for structuring abbreviations are contained in **Rule 6**. Specific abbreviations are compiled as follows:

- Table T1 contains abbreviations for **federal and state courts and reporters**, divided up by jurisdiction.

- Table T6 contains words that are always abbreviated in **case names in citations**.

- Table T7 provides general abbreviations for various **courts** (not jurisdiction specific - for that see Table T1).

- Table T8 contains abbreviations for **explanatory phrases used in a case's prior and subsequent history**.

- Table T9 provides abbreviations for **legislative documents**.

- Table T10 provides abbreviations for **geographical terms**.

- Table T11 provides abbreviations for the **titles of judges and other officials**.

- Table T12 provides abbreviations for the **months of the year**.

- Table T13 provides abbreviations for **journals and other periodicals**.

*   *   *

Spacing[23]

Spaces are key components in abbreviations. The general rule is this: when stringing abbreviations together, always surround multiple letter abbreviations with spaces (spaces are shown by the dot). So:

```
F.•Supp.•2d
Mich.•Ct.•App.
S.•Ct.
```

In contrast, a string of single letter abbreviations contains no spaces. So:

```
S.D.N.Y
F.3d
```

And finally, a combination of the two looks like this:

```
E.D.•Pa.
N.D.•Cal.
```

*   *   *

Signals and Parentheticals

Signals

Signals introduce legal citations whether in text or footnotes.[24] They explain the manner in which the citation supports the proposition. If **[no signal]** is used, that means that the proposition in the cited authority and the author's proposition are the same. So, **[no signal]** is always used when **quoting** from a source and also when the proposition noted in the source and the proposition made by the author are identical.

The most common signals are listed below and each is discussed separately. Each discussion also contains an example of the typeface used for each signal when used in law review footnotes and when used in court documents and legal memoranda.

Please note that the first letter of a signal is only capitalized when the signal begins a citation sentence.

*   *   *

E.g.,

When you use **e.g.,** to introduce a citation, you are saying that there are multiple sources that state the **same** proposition as the one you are making in your

---

[24]   For more information on signals, see *Bluebook* Rule 1.2.

paper, but citing to all of them would be superfluous (so you only cite to one and introduce it with **e.g.,**).

E.g., typeface examples can be found below.

Law Review Footnotes

E.g.,

Court Documents and Legal Memoranda

<u>E.g.,</u>

Please note that when using this signal, the final comma is neither italicized in a law review footnote nor underlined in court documents and legal memoranda.

*   *   *

See

When you use **see,** you are stating that the cited authority "clearly supports"[25] your proposition. According to *The Bluebook*, **see** is used rather than **[no   signal]** when your proposition is **not** identical to that stated by the cited authority, but, nevertheless, follows obviously from it.[26]

---

[25]   BLUEBOOK, *supra* note 5, at 54.

[26]   *See id.*

Typeface examples are below.

Law Review Footnotes

See

Court Documents and Legal Memoranda

<u>See</u>

Please note: there is no comma between **see** and the citation.

In addition to using **see** as an introductory signal, it may also be used in a citation as a verb. In that case, **see** is neither underlined nor italicized. An example is below.

For additional discussion of the Venerable Bede's philosophy, see *supra* note 8 and accompanying text.

*   *   *

See also

When you use **see also**, you are stating that the authority you are citing is **additional** authority in support of your proposition, and that you have already "cited or discussed" authority that **states or directly supports** the proposition.[27] You should use an explanatory parenthetical[28] with **see also**.

---

[27]   *Id.*

The typefaces for **see also** are the same as those for **see**.

*   *   *

See, e.g.,

See, e.g., is an awesome little invention. As a combination of **e.g.,** and **see**, it is used when many authorities support, **but do not directly state**, your proposition, and when citation to all of them would not be helpful.

Typeface examples are below.

Law Review Footnotes

See, e.g., Bell Atlantic Corp. v. Twombly, 550 U.S. 544, 553 (2007).

Court Documents and Legal Memoranda

See, e.g., Bell Atlantic Corp. v. Twombly, 550 U.S. 544, 553 (2007).

Please note: the *second period* in **see, e.g.,** is italicized in a law review footnote and underlined in court documents and legal memoranda. The *second comma*, however, is not.

---

[28]   For more on explanatory parentheticals, see pages 26-27.

Accord

When you use **accord**, you are stating that you are citing to two or more sources that "**state** or **clearly support**" your proposition, but your "text quotes or refers to only one."[29] In that case, the source referred to in your text is introduced with [**no signal**] or **see**, and immediately thereafter, the additional sources are introduced with **accord**.

See below for an example using the different typefaces.

Law Review Footnotes

Miller v. Pepper, 638 P.2d 864, 868 (Haw. Ct. App. 1982); *accord* Brewer v. Michigan Salt Ass'n, 11 N.W. 370, 373 (Mich. 1882).

Court Documents and Legal Memoranda

Miller v. Pepper, 638 P.2d 864, 868 (Haw. Ct. App. 1982); accord Brewer v. Michigan Salt Ass'n, 11 N.W. 370, 373 (Mich. 1882).

---

[29]   *Id.*

Cf.

Cf. is the abbreviation for **compare**. When you use **cf.** to introduce a citation, you are stating that the authority you are citing supports a proposition **different** than yours, but which is nevertheless "sufficiently analogous to lend support."[30] You should include an explanatory parenthetical when using **cf.**

The typeface is the same as that for **see**, but make sure to <u>underline</u> the period in court documents and legal memoranda and *italicize* it in law review footnotes!

*   *   *

Contra

Use **contra** when the source "***directly states the contrary* of the proposition**" you are making.[31] The typeface conventions for **contra** are exactly like those for **see**.

*   *   *

---

[30]   *Id.* at 55.

[31]   *Id.* (emphasis added).

But see

Who doesn't love **but see**? Use **but see** when the source you are citing "clearly supports a proposition *contrary*" to yours.[32] The typeface conventions for **but see** are exactly like those for **see**.

*　　*　　*

See generally

Use **see generally** when the source cited provides helpful <u>background</u> information related to your proposition.[33] An explanatory parenthetical when using **see generally** is often helpful. The typeface conventions for **see generally** are exactly like those for **see**.

*　　*　　*

A Final Note on Signals

When stringing together citations that are introduced by different signals, please remember two important things: (1) Insert semicolons between citations that are introduced by the same type of signal (that is, signals that *support* a proposition are of one type, and signals that *contradict* a proposition are of another type). Citations that are introduced

---

[32]   *Id.* (emphasis added).

[33]   *Id.*

[25]

by signals of a different type are separated by periods. (2) When a signal follows a semicolon, it is <u>not</u> capitalized. When the signal follows a period, it is capitalized. An example is below (with the signals **bolded** for clarity).

> ***See*** Miller v. Pepper, 638 P.2d 864, 868 (Haw. Ct. App. 1982); ***see also*** Brewer v. Michigan Salt Ass'n, 11 N.W. 370, 373 (Mich. 1882). ***But see*** City of Miami v. Spicy, 284 So.2d 699 (Fla. Ct. App. 1973).

*　　*　　*

Parentheticals

Parentheticals are explanatory comments that follow a citation and explain in detail why you are citing the resource in question. Usage of an explanatory parenthetical depends on the introductory signal used.

There is no need to supply a **parenthetical** when you are using [**no signal**], **e.g.**, or **contra** because the relevance of the citation is readily apparent from the signal alone (look above in the discussions of the specific signals to see why this is so). Usage of other signals, however, may require a bit more explanation. In this vein, you should <u>consider</u> supplying a parenthetical when introducing citations with **accord**; **see**; **see, e.g.,**; and **but see**, as the relevance of your citation may not be readily apparent, and *The Bluebook* practically <u>requires</u> the use of parentheticals when using the signals **see also**, **cf.**, and **see generally**, because in those situations, the relevance of the specific citation is likely <u>not</u> apparent from the signal alone.

Parenthetical explanations generally begin with a present participle (the "ing" form of a verb) like "discussing," "arguing," "holding," "explaining," etc. Examples are below.

> The Supreme Court has long deferred to Congress on matters pertaining to major league baseball. <u>See, e.g.</u>, <u>Flood v. Kuhn</u>, 407 U.S. 258 (1972) (holding that change in baseball's antitrust exemption must come from Congress, not the courts).

> Because of the danger they present to livestock, Massachusetts should require that all pet pot-bellied pigs be properly licensed. <u>Cf.</u> Mass. Gen. Laws ch. 140, § 137 (2010) (implying that purpose of dog licensing requirement is to control dog and restrain it from "killing, chasing, or harassing live stock").

For additional information on explanatory parentheticals, see *Bluebook* Rule 1.5.

*   *   *

Citing Cases

Generally

Cases that are published in print reporters are always cited in the same way, whether you find them in the actual book or online (that is, cases are always cited as if you found them in print). The elements of the citation are below. The commas are in the correct places.

[case name], [volume number] [abbreviated name of print reporter] [page number on which the case begins], [pincite] [(court that decided the case and year of decision)].

*   *   *

Reporters

A **reporter** is a set of books in which cases from a particular jurisdiction or collection of jurisdictions are published in print. Cases are always identified by volume number of the reporter in which they appear, the reporter's abbreviation, and the page number on which the case begins. So, by way of example, **17 F.3d 660** refers to the case that begins on page 660 of volume 17 of the Federal Reporter 3d Series[34] (which collects cases from the federal courts of appeals).

---

[34] A "series" is a complete set of volumes of a reporter, covering a set time period. There are three "series" of the Federal Reporter. The first numbered 300 volumes; the second 999 volumes; and the third is now over 700 volumes.

Federal reporters and their abbreviations are shown below, with regional reporters (which collect state cases) on the page following.

Federal Reporters

Reporter	Years Covered	Abbreviation
District Court		
Federal Supplement	1932-1998	F. Supp.
Federal Supplement 2d	1998-date	F. Supp. 2d
Federal Rules Decisions	1938-date	F.R.D.
West's Bankruptcy Reporter	1979-date	B.R.
Circuit Court		
Federal Reporter	1891-1924	F.
Federal Reporter 2d	1924-1993	F.2d
Federal Reporter 3d	1993-date	F.3d
Federal Appendix (unpub cases)	2001-date	F. App'x
Supreme Court		
United States Reports (official reporter)	1790-date	U.S.
Supreme Court Reporter (unofficial; published by West)	1882-date	S. Ct.
Lawyer's Edition (unofficial; published by Lexis)	1790-date	L. Ed., L. Ed. 2d

Regional (State) Reporters

Reporter	Abbreviation	States Covered
Atlantic	A., A.2d, A.3d	CT, DC, DE, MD, ME, NH, NJ, PA, RI, VT
North Eastern	N.E., N.E.2d	IL, IN, MA, NY, OH
North Western	N.W., N.W.2d	IA, MI, MN, ND, NE, SD, WI
Pacific	P., P.2d, P.3d	AK, AZ, CA, CO, HI, ID, KS, MT, NM, NV, OK, OR, UT, WA, WY
Southern	So., So. 2d, So. 3d	AL, FL, LA, MS
South Eastern	S.E., S.E.2d	GA, NC, SC, VA, WV
South Western	S.W., S.W.2d, S.W.3d	AR, KY, MO, TN, TX

Abbreviations in Case Names

For case names in citations, abbreviate any word listed in Table T6 and geographical units listed in Table T10, unless the geographical unit is a party.

When using case names in textual sentences, only abbreviate well known acronyms, such as CIA, FBI, etc. and the following eight words: **&, Ass'n, Bros., Co., Corp., Inc., Ltd., and No.**

*　　　*　　　*

Case Name

In court documents and legal memoranda, case names are <u>underlined</u>. The examples below are for case names in citations contained within law review footnotes, in which the case name is not underlined (case names in the text of law review footnotes are *italicized*). The dot shows where a space should be inserted. Please note how "FDIC" is abbreviated pursuant to Rule 6.

```
Bateman•v.•FDIC,•[citation].
```

For the state case below, please note how the words "Markets" and "Federal" and "Incorporated" are abbreviated pursuant to Table T6.

```
Acme•Mkts.,•Inc.•v.•Fed.•Armored•
Express,•Inc.,•[citation].
```

*　　　*　　　*

Parallel Citations

A parallel citation contains citation to where a case appears in the West regional reporter <u>and</u> to where it appears in the official state reporter.

Parallel citations only apply with regard to documents submitted to a *state court* and only then when dictated by *local rule*, which will identify the official state reporter(s) to which citation must be made. Otherwise, use the regional reporter only in your citation (with the appropriate abbreviation to the state court in the parenthetical).

If you are going to use a parallel citation, structure it by citing to the official state reporter first and then to the regional reporter. Pincites are given for both reporters if appropriate. An example is below.

<u>Strongman v. Idaho Potato Comm'n</u>, 129 Idaho 766, 771, 932 P.2d 889, 895 (1992).

* * *

Case Citation Information

Immediately following the case name comes the case citation information. Abbreviations are important here too; particularly for the relevant reporter and court. For federal court abbreviations and citation formats, see the beginning of Table T1 (United States Jurisdictions). The citation below is from a United States district court case from the District of Massachusetts. **Please take note of the spacing.**

112·F.·Supp.·2d·89·(D.·Mass.·2000)

Key to Citation

112 = Volume Number
F. Supp. 2d = Reporter in which the case is
published in print
89 = Page on which the case begins
D. Mass. = Court that decided the case
2000 = Year the case was decided

This case is found in the volume of the Federal Supplement 2d reporter shown below.

Here's a citation to a case from the United States
Court of Appeals for the Third Circuit.

```
157•F.3d•191•(3d•Cir.•1998)
```

> **Key to Citation**
>
> 157 = Volume Number
> F.3d = Reporter in which the case is published
> in print
> 191 = Page on which the case begins
> 3d Cir. = Court that decided the case
> 1998 = Year the case was decided

This case is found in the volume of the Federal
Reporter 3d shown below.

For state court abbreviations and citation formats, see Table T1 (states are listed alphabetically). With state cases, citation to the regional reporter <u>only</u> is generally preferred (no parallel cites). The citation below is from the intermediate appellate court in Pennsylvania (see Table T1 for the court's abbreviation). The elements of the citation are the same as those of a federal case.

```
648·A.2d·1218·(Pa.·Super.·Ct.·1994).
```

This case is found in the volume of the Atlantic Reporter 2d shown below.

Unpublished Cases

With the exception of federal appellate cases that appear in the *Federal Appendix*, **unpublished** cases are those cases that do not appear in a print reporter. These cases are generally cited as they appear in Westlaw and LexisNexis. Please see the examples below.

Westlaw Example.

```
Gonzales-Doldan·v.·ABPS,·No.·97-CV-
0902E,·1998·WL·328642,·at·*1·
(W.D.N.Y.·June·16,·1998).
```

Key to Citation

No. 97-CV-0902E = Docket Number
1998 WL 328642 = Westlaw Identifier
*1 = Pin Cite
W.D.N.Y. = Court
June 16, 1998 = Date of Decision

Please note that the actual date that the case was decided, and not just the year, is used with unpublished cases. Please also note that in unpublished cases, page numbers are always accompanied by an asterisk [*]. This is called "star-paging."

LexisNexis Example.

```
Del. Express Shuttle, Inc. v.
Older, No. 19596, 2002 Del. Ch.
LEXIS 124, at *16 (Del. Ch.
Oct. 23, 2002).
```

Key to Citation

```
No. 19596
```
= Docket Number

```
2002 Del. Ch. LEXIS 124
```
= LexisNexis Identifier

`*16` = Pin Cite

`Del. Ch.` = Court

`Oct. 23, 2002` = Date of Decision

For more information on unpublished cases, see *Bluebook* Rule 10.8.1.

*   *   *

Final Note on Citing Cases: For cases where the citation to the reporter clearly identifies the court (for example, Flood v. Kuhn, 407 U.S. 258 (1972)), there is no need to identify the deciding court in the parenthetical.

*   *   *

Citing Statutes

Generally

Statutes are laws passed by legislative bodies, whether federal or state. The federal legislature—the United States Congress—passes laws during legislative sessions. Each session lasts two years.

Statutes are generally published in two forms, first as a session law and then as a code. The session law is the law or act exactly as passed by the legislature. Session laws at the federal level are published in chronological order of passage in the *United States Statutes at Large*. The federal session laws are called *public laws*, and identified as follows: **Public Law No. 111-148**, which refers to the 148th law passed in the 111th session of Congress. Most federal session laws have a name, like, for example, the Immigration and Naturalization Act of 1952 (INA). This name is known as the session law's popular name. Federal session laws are also identified by where they are published in the Statutes at Large; for example, **61 Stat. 637**.

Because session laws are published in chronological order and likely contain sections involving different subject areas, they do not lend themselves to efficient legal research. For that reason, following passage by the legislature, a session law is *codified* and placed in a *code*, like, for example, the *United States Code* (U.S.C.). Codes are organized by subject.

Citing statutes can be difficult as the formats differ between federal and state, and from state to state.

Citation formats also differ as between codes and session laws.

You must always check *Bluebook* Table T1 to find the correct citation format when citing to a particular jurisdiction's statutes.

For more information on citing to statutes, see *Bluebook* Rule 12.

Because of the state-by-state variance in statutory code structure, this section of the *Quick Guide* will, for the most part, focus on the United States Code only.[35] Please understand that the citation principles discussed with regard to the federal code are directly applicable to state code citations as well.

* * *

Structure of the United States Code

The United States Code (U.S.C.) is organized by subject and comprised of 51 Titles. A Title is not a volume number, but rather corresponds to a subject area. The 51 Titles are as follows:

---

[35] Generally, proper citation to the United States Code is to the official unannotated version, the U.S.C.; not to the unofficial annotated versions, the U.S.C.A. and the U.S.C.S. *See* BLUEBOOK Rule 12.3.

[40]

- TITLE 44 - PUBLIC PRINTING AND DOCUMENTS
- TITLE 45 - RAILROADS
- TITLE 46 - SHIPPING
- TITLE 47 - TELEGRAPHS, TELEPHONES, AND RADIOTELEGRAPHS
- TITLE 48 - TERRITORIES AND INSULAR POSSESSIONS
- TITLE 49 - TRANSPORTATION
- TITLE 50 - WAR AND NATIONAL DEFENSE
- TITLE 51 - NATIONAL AND COMMERCIAL SPACE PROGRAMS

As is the U.S.C. as a whole, each Title is organized by subject and divided up into Parts, Chapters, and Sections.

Proper citation to the U.S.C. requires the relevant title number, section number, and year of publication of the code in print.

A proper citation is below.

                42 U.S.C. § 1983 (2012).

42 is the title number, **1983** is the section number, and **2012** in the parenthetical is the year of publication of the code in print. Of the three elements to the citation, the year of publication of the code in print is by far the most difficult to ascertain.

                *   *   *

Year of Publication of the Code in Print

The correct year of publication to use when citing to a code section is the year of publication of the last **official print** edition of the code, provided that

[41]

your code section has not been enacted or amended **since** the last official edition was published.[36] The official edition of the U.S.C. is published every six years and the latest official edition is from 2012. The official editions of state codes are published at more frequent intervals. For example, the official version of the codified General Laws of Massachusetts is published every two years.

To find the correct year of publication of a code (federal or state), look at the following, in this order of preference: (1) the spine of the book, (2) the title page, and (3) the copyright page. For the U.S.C., the correct year is on the spine of the book. **You must refer to the print volume in order to find the correct year.**

---

[36]   There is an exception to this in *Bluebook* rule 12.5, which permits citation to codes found in online databases without reference to the year of the code found in print. This exception has very little impact on law students, however. In law school, and in particular with regard to law journals, use of the year of the code as found in print is almost always preferred to that found online.

Below is a photo of a pair of volumes of the United States Code showing the year of publication on the spines of the books.

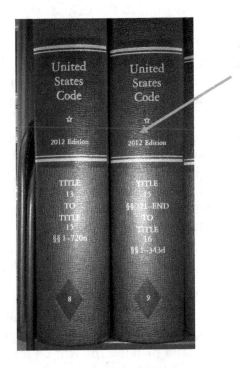

You will use the year of the most recent official edition of the code (as noted, for the U.S.C. that year is 2012) *alone* in the parenthetical of your citation if the code section you are citing was in existence as of that year *and has not been changed since.*

How to tell whether your code section has changed since the most recent official edition of the code? Easy. Find your code section on Westlaw or Lexis. At the conclusion of the statutory text you will find something called **Credits** or **History**. This will show you when the statute was enacted and all the times it has been amended. Below is an example of the credits/history from **26 U.S.C. § 280H**.

> (Added *Dec. 22, 1987*, P.L. 100-203, Title X, § 10206(c)(1), 101 Stat. 1330-401; *Nov. 10, 1988*, P.L. 100-647, Title II, § 2004(e)(2)(B), (3), (14)(A), (C), 102 Stat. 3600, 3602.) [my emphasis].

This tells you that § 280H was enacted on December 22, 1987; amended on November 10, 1988; and has not been changed since 1988. Therefore, when citing to § 280H, the proper year of the U.S.C. to use is 2012 because the section was in existence as of then and has not been changed since. Thus:

```
26 U.S.C. § 280H (2012).
```

If your code section was in existence as of the last official year of publication and has been amended **since** then, you must look in a supplement or pocket part, and then use the year on the spine, title page, or copyright page of the supplement or pocket part in addition to using the year of the last official publication

In between the years of publication of the official edition of the U.S.C. (2000, 2006, 2012, etc.), the federal government publishes annual Supplements that include changes made to the U.S.C. since the last official edition.

The supplements are identified with a year and with a roman numeral.

A photo showing the spines of a pair of volumes of the Supplement is below.

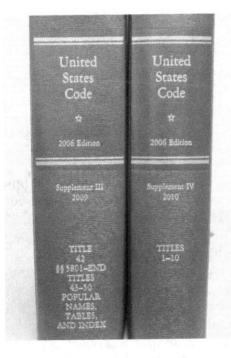

The photo shows a volume from Supplement III for 2009 and one from Supplement IV for 2010. Remember, these are supplements to the 2006 official edition of the U.S.C., showing changes to the code made subsequent to 2006. If the 2012 edition of the U.S.C. had not yet been released and we needed to cite to a code section that had been amended or enacted in, say, 2010, we would need to cite to an annual supplement of the 2006 edition of the code in one of the two following forms.

If the code section was in existence in 2006 and only amended in 2010.

```
26 U.S.C. § 302 (2006 & Supp. IV
                2010).
```

If the code section was not in existence in 2006 and enacted for this first time in 2010.

```
16 U.S.C. § 3645(d)(2) (Supp. IV
                2010).
```

There have been as of yet no supplements issued since publication of the 2012 edition of the United States Code.

Because there are not, as of yet, any supplements to the 2012 edition of the U.S.C., if the section we are citing was amended or enacted after 2012, we need to cite to the U.S.C.A., a West publication, rather than to the official U.S.C. or to any U.S.C. supplement. As of April 2014, the U.S.C.A. is current through December 2013.

A sample citation to the U.S.C.A. is below. The year of publication for U.S.C.A. hardbound volumes is found on the copyright page.

```
42 U.S.C.A. § 7513 (West 2013).
```

Citing to an Entire Statute in a Code

When citing to an entire statute as found in a code, as opposed to an individual section of the code, every section of the statute is referenced. For guidance, use the following as examples.

```
Securities Act of 1933, 15 U.S.C. §§ 77a-77aa (2012).

Aircraft Safety Act of 2000, 18 U.S.C. § 38 (2012).
```

*   *   *

Session Laws

A session law is the law as it is passed by the legislature, before it is divided up by subject area and codified in the appropriate place in a code.

When citing to a federal session law, always include the following information: Name of Legislation (omit "The" as first word of name), public law or chapter number, Statutes at Large citation, and year of legislation if not already apparent from the statute's name. Examples of session law citation are below.

```
Sherwood Act, ch. 123, 37 Stat. 112 (1912).
```

```
Clean•Water•Act•of•1977,•Pub.•L.•No.•
95-217,•91•Stat.•1566.
```

*   *   *

State Statutes

Statutory Codes

State code citation format is **always** jurisdiction-specific. You must check the relevant state's section in Table T1 of *The Bluebook* in order to cite the code correctly. Examples are below. Please note the usage of large and small caps in law review footnotes.

Massachusetts

Law Review Footnotes

```
Mass.•Gen.•Laws•ch.•x,•§•x•(<year>).
```

Court Documents

```
Mass.•Gen.•Laws•ch.•x,•§•x•(<year>).
```

New York

Law Review Footnotes

```
N.Y.•Banking•Law•§•x•(McKinney•<year>).
```

Court Documents

```
N.Y.•Banking•Law•§•x•(McKinney•<year>).
```

Session Laws

Like state codified laws, proper citation to state session laws is jurisdiction-specific (although all state session law citations share some common elements). Please make sure to check Table T1. An example from Massachusetts is below.

```
Act•of•July•8,•2011,•ch.•65,•
2011•Mass.•Legis.•Serv.•76•(West).
```

Please note that although the proper citation format varies from state to state, every citation to a state session law must contain the name of the legislation (the "Act of ..." construction is used when there is no popular name), a ch.# or other #, and then the appropriate cite to the proper bound volume where the session law was initially published.

*   *   *

Citing Secondary Sources

A secondary source is a source that is *about* the law rather than the actual law itself. Secondary sources come in many different varieties, from dictionaries and single volume monographs to journal articles, legal encyclopedias and practice guides. The various types of secondary sources have somewhat different citation formats. The most common types and formats are discussed below.

*   *   *

Year of Publication for Secondary Sources

Proper citation to secondary sources requires the year of publication of the *print* version. For periodicals like law reviews and newspapers, this is not a problem as the year of publication of the print version is supplied online.

For non-periodical secondary sources, like Massachusetts Practice, dictionaries, and legal encyclopedias, the year of publication of the print version is not available online and you must use the actual print volume to find it (the year is usually on the copyright page).

*   *   *

Dictionaries

Everyone knows dictionaries are awesome. Cite them according to the examples below, noting again the difference in formats between law review footnotes and court documents and legal memoranda.

Law Review Footnotes

BLACK'S•LAW•DICTIONARY•65•(9th•ed.•2009).

RANDOM•HOUSE•COLLEGE•DICTIONARY•643•(8th•ed.•1984).

Court Documents

Black's•Law•Dictionary•65•(9th•ed.•2009).

Random•House•College•Dictionary•643•(8th•ed.•1984).

For dictionaries, the proper year of publication can only be found in the print volume.

*   *   *

Legal Encyclopedias

Everyone loves a good legal encyclopedia. Cite them according to the examples below.

Law Review Footnotes

1•Aм.•Jur.•2d•*Accession•&•Confusion*•§•
15•(2005).

35A•C.J.S.•*Federal•Civil•Procedure*•§
•318•(2003).

Court Documents

1•Am.•Jur.•2d•<u>Accession•&•Confusion</u>•§
•15•(2005).

35A•C.J.S.•<u>Federal•Civil•Procedure</u>•§
•318•(2003).

For legal encyclopedias, the proper year of publication can only be found in the print volume.

Journals and Periodicals

Consecutively Paginated. Cite consecutively paginated[37] journal articles with reference to the example below. The key is to use the correct abbreviation for whatever journal you are citing. You can find the abbreviations for just about any law journal you can imagine in *The Bluebook* at Table T13.

> Samuel•D.•Warren•&•Louis•D.•Brandeis,•*The• Right•to•Privacy*,•4•HARV.•L.•REV.•193•(1890).

Please note: The above citation is proper for law review footnotes. The title of the article is *italicized* and the abbreviated name of the journal is in LARGE AND SMALL CAPS. When appearing in court documents or legal memoranda, by contrast, the title of the article is underlined and the abbreviation of the journal is written in ordinary roman type.

Non-Consecutively Paginated. Cite journals and periodicals that are separately paginated within each issue according to the examples below.

> Mary•Beard,•*Alexander:•How•Great?*,•N.Y.•REV.• BOOKS,•Oct.•27,•2011,•at•35.

> Michael•Scherer,•*Taking•it•to•the• Streets*,•TIME,•Oct.•24,•2011,•at 20.

---

[37]   These are journals that are consecutively paginated throughout an entire volume, with each issue's beginning page number starting where the previous issue left off.

Newspapers are generally cited the same way as non-consecutively paginated journals.

```
Nick•Cafardo,•Cardinals•Force•Game•7,•
BOSTON•GLOBE,•Oct.•28,•2011,•at•C1.

Holland•Cotter,•A•Cosmopolitan•Trove•of•
Exotic•Beauty,•N.Y.•TIMES,•Oct.•28,•2011,
•at•C23.
```

As always with periodicals, change italics to underlining and large and small caps to regular roman type when citing in court documents and legal memoranda.

*   *   *

American Law Reports (A.L.R.)

Cite American Law Reports according to *Bluebook* Rule 16.7.6.

Law Review Footnotes

```
Fern•L.•Kletter,•Annotation,•Validity,
•Construction,•and•Application•of•
Statutes•Prohibiting•Boating•While•
Under•the•Influence,•or•the•Like,•47•
A.L.R.6th•107•(2009).
```

Court Documents

Fern•L.•Kletter,•Annotation,•<u>Validity,</u>
•<u>Construction,•and•Application•of•</u>
<u>Statutes•Prohibiting•Boating•While•</u>
<u>Under•the•Influence,•or•the•Like</u>,•47•
A.L.R.6th•107•(2009).

If the A.L.R. annotation to which you are citing does not have a named author, simply begin the citation with the word "Annotation."

The proper year of publication for A.L.R. is available online through Westlaw Next or in print.

Massachusetts Practice

Massachusetts Practice is tricky. Cite it according to *Bluebook* rule 15.8. An example, showing the proper citation format for both law review footnotes and court documents is below.

Law Review Footnotes

35A•Mass.•Practice•*Consumer•Law*•§•10:37•
(2010).

Court Documents

35A•Mass.•Practice•<u>Consumer•Law</u>•§•
10:37•(2010).

Please note: You can find the subject area ("Consumer Law") on the front or spine of the volume. The year of publication is on the copyright page of the print volume.

Please see the next page for a photo of the volume noted above.

*   *   *

Find the year of publication inside the volume, on the copyright page.

Multi-Volume Treatises

Cite multi-volume treatises in law review footnotes like the example below.

> 4 CHARLES ALAN WRIGHT & ARTHUR R. MILLER, FEDERAL PRACTICE AND PROCEDURE § 1006 (2d ed. 1987).

Below is a more complex citation that refers to a shorter work published in a multi-volume treatise.

> Saul Cornell & Gerald Leonard, *The Consolidation of the Early Federal System, 1791-1812, in* 1 CAMBRIDGE HISTORY OF LAW IN AMERICA 518 (Michael Grossberg & Christopher Tomlins eds., 2008).

There's a lot going on in this citation, so we've omitted the space indicators to make it easier to read. First, as noted above, this is not just a citation to a multi-volume treatise. Rather, it's a cite to a shorter, independently authored, work that is contained within a multi-volume treatise. The shorter work is cited as it was an article, and the multi-volume treatise is as if it was a book, with the "1" before the treatise title being the relevant volume number.

*　　　*　　　*

Single Volume Treatises and Monographs

In law review footnotes, cite books and other single volume treatises or monographs like the example below. For non-academic purposes, change everything to regular roman type except the book's title, which is underlined.

DANIEL•WALKER•HOWE, •WHAT•HATH•GOD•
WROUGHT:•THE•TRANSFORMATION•OF•AMERICA,
•1815-48•141•(2007).

*   *   *

Citing to Pocket Parts
and Other Supplements

Remember, the rule is that if the source you are citing is available in print, you must cite to it as if you found it in print. This means that from time to time **when citing to certain secondary sources and statutory codes**, you will need to cite to material in a pocket part or supplement.

Citing to material in a pocket part or supplement does not affect the main citation; it only impacts the year of publication.

So, for an example regarding a state statute, chapter 111N, section 2 of the Massachusetts General Laws was in existence as of the last official year of the code (2010) and has been amended since. That means material will be found in both the main volume and the supplement.

If the statute was only found in the main volume, its citation would look like this (in a court document):

```
Mass. Gen. Laws ch. 111N, § 2 (2010)
```

However, because the statute is found in both the main volume and the supplement, the citation looks like this:

```
Mass. Gen. Laws ch. 111N, § 2 (2010 &
            Supp. 2012)
```

The main volume and the supplement are shown below.

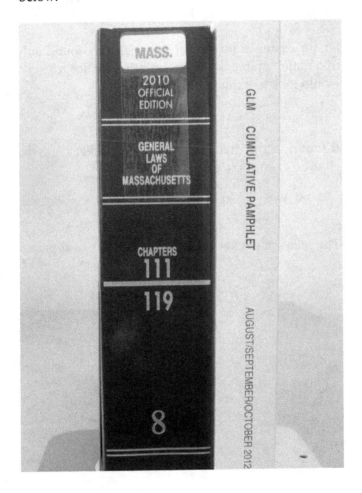

The same thing must be done with certain secondary sources like Massachusetts Practice, legal encyclopedias, and A.L.R.

So, for example, if relevant material were found only in a main volume of Massachusetts Practice, the cite would look like this:

```
35A Mass. Practice Consumer Law § 10:37 (2010).
```

If found in the main volume and a pocket part, the citation changes to this:

```
35A Mass. Practice Consumer Law § 10:37 (2010 & Supp. 2012).
```

The relevant pocket part is shown on the next page.

MASSACHUSETTS PRACTICE SERIES™

Volume 35A

Consumer Law
THIRD EDITION

2012-2013 Pocket Part
Issued in September 2012

By
THOMAS B. MERRITT
of the Massachusetts Bar

Chapters 8 to 19

WEST.
A Thomson Reuters business

For Customer Assistance Call 1-800-328-4880

Mat #41168700

Short Citation Forms

A short citation form is a shorthand method for referring to a citation that has already been cited in full.

The most common short form is <u>id.</u> <u>Id.</u> is used to cite to the "immediately preceding authority," but solely when the immediately preceding citation or footnote contains one authority only.[38]

Other short forms are simply shorter versions of the full citation. The general rule is that use of a short form is appropriate in **academic citation** if the short form clearly identifies the resource cited to and the resource is already cited (in either full or short form) in the same footnote or one of the preceding **five** footnotes.[39] For **non-academic purposes**, use of the short form is appropriate when it clearly identifies the resource cited to, the full citation form appears in the same general discussion, and the reader will not have trouble locating the full cite.[40]

For examples of appropriate short forms for cases and statutes, see *Bluebook* Rules 10.9 (cases) and 12.10 (statutes). For examples of appropriate short

---

[38]   BLUEBOOK, *supra* note 5, at 72.

[39]   *See, e.g., id.* at 72.

[40]   *See, e.g., id.* at 13.

forms for other types of resources, see *Bluebook* Rule 4.2.

*   *   *

Conclusion

This *Quick Guide* is short, on purpose. To go into much more detail, I believe, would result in a *Bluebook* clone and defeat the essential purpose of this project, which is to provide simple answers to the basic citation questions faced by new law students. To this end, and without rehashing specific citation rules, the key points to remember are these:

- Be aware of the Essential Bluebooking Tips discussed at the outset of the book.

- Are your citations for use in law review footnotes (that is, for academic purposes) or in court documents or legal memoranda (that is, for non-academic purposes)? Know which one and cite accordingly.

- To use the proper signal, make sure you know why you are citing to a particular source.

- Be aware that *The Bluebook* will almost always supply you with the proper abbreviation, whether it's for a case name, the name of a court, the name of a reporter, the name of a journal, etc.

- When citing to a particular source, try to find an example in *The Bluebook* to copy from; it's easier than trying to read and apply a rule.

- Always ask questions if you need help. Good Luck!

*   *   *

Additional Reading

Not everyone loves the Bluebook. Below find some friendly and not-so-friendly critiques.

- Richard A. Posner, *The* Bluebook *Blues*, 120 YALE L.J. 850 (2011).
- Warren D. Rees, *Singing the* Bluebook *Blues*, 1 AALL SPECTRUM 20 (June 1997).
- James W. Paulsen, *An Uninformed System of Citation*, 105 HARV. L. REV. 1780 (1992).
- James D. Gordon III, *Oh No! A New* Bluebook!, 90 MICH. L. REV. 1698 (1992).
- Jim Chen, *Something Old, Something New, Something Borrowed, Something Blue*, 58 U. CHI. L. REV. 1527 (1991).
- Richard A. Posner, *Goodbye to the* Bluebook, 53 U. CHI. L. REV. 1343 (1986).
- Arnold B. Kanter, *Putting Your Best Footnote Forward*, BARRISTER (Spring 1982) at 42.
- Kevin C. Gralley & John C. Aisenbrey, Book Note, 65 GEO. L.J. 871 (1977).
- Alan Strasser, *Technical Due Process*, 12 HARV. C.L.-C.R. REV. 507 (1977).
- Peter Lushing, Book Review, 67 COLUM. L. REV. 599 (1967).

And the editors of the Bluebook have responded.

- Book Note, *Manual Labor, Chicago Style*, 101 HARV. L. REV. 1323 (1988).